Arturo's Studio
Presents

Destin, Florida
Highway to Heaven

Vintage Photography
by Arturo Mennillo

Dedication

*Dedicated to my father, Arturo Mennillo.
Without his life's work, this book
would not have been possible.*

Dedicated to my family....

*This book is also dedicated to the Village of Destin and
its founders and residents, who with grace, respect and
determination have lived in nature's flow.*

— Anthony A. Mennillo

Copyright © 1998. All rights reserved. No part of this book may be reproduced or transmitted in any form or by any means, electronic or mechanical, including photocopying and recording or by any information storage or retrieval system without prior written permission from Arturo's Studio and the publisher, except for brief passages in a review or article about the book

ISBN: 0-9667885-0-8

First Edition: September 1998

Publisher's Cataloging in Publication

Highway to Heaven, Destin, Florida - Vintage Photography by Arturo Mennillo / Anthony A. Mennillo

Stories (unless credited) as told by Captain Reddin (Salty) Brunson

Short Stories:
An Emerald Coast Deed To Remember, written by: James Keir Baughman

Special thanks to: Marianne & Ward S. Merrick, Jr., founders of the Northwest Florida
Emerald Coast Storytelling Guild

All inquiries regarding the images included in this book of photography
and all other works by Arturo may be directed to Arturo's Studio.

Printed and bound in the United States of America.

Production Credits

Author: Tony Mennillo

Copy Editor: Judy Adamski

Production Manager: Joe Adamski

Production Coordinator: Bill Morgan

Book Designer: Tony Mennillo, Judy Adamski

Cover Design: Judy Adamski

Assistant to the Author: Sharon Mennillo

Proofreader: Sandy Brabon

Contributing Writers: Reddin Brunson, James Keir Baughman, O. T. Melvin, Percy Hamilton

Photography: Arturo Mennillo

Arturo's Studio

in conjunction with

The Destin Library

present

an Interactive Tour of the Emerald Coast.
This CD-Rom features Arturo's photography along with
narration by some of the area's pioneers.

The CD-Rom is now on sale.

The images you are enjoying in this book
are available through Arturo's Studio.
Sizes range from 8" x 10" to 40" x 50".

For more information contact us at:

Arturo's Studio
380 Bayou Circle
Freeport, Florida 32439
(850) 835-7737

Olivia and Arturo Mennillo

Acknowledgments

My great grandparents, Lorenzo and Etta Brown Brunson, left Boggy Bayou area and came across the Choctawhatchee Bay to settle in Destin in 1926. I, like many of my friends after college, left the area in pursuit of higher paying corporate jobs. When I left in 1972 at the age of 22, it was with great sadness. I was born here. I swam and fished in the blue-green waters, and played on the snow white beaches and dunes throughout my childhood. I was immersed in Destin socially, creatively and emotionally. I was as captivated by its tropical beauty and bittersweet history as any native son or daughter.

My wife, Sharon, and I remained in Florida sailing and fishing the many nooks and crannies of this wonderful state. Still, we found no place with the abundance of natural resources as in Destin. As we moved around, our friends grew in number and diversity - ranging from sea captains, fishermen, corporate executives and land developers to ministers, northwest Florida storytellers, teachers, and volunteers. These are the people I thought about again and again in writing this book.

As for the people I wish to thank, it is impossible to list them all by name, just as I cannot cite every name of the many fish in the Gulf. At the top of this list is my wife, Sharon, who has encouraged me in everything I have ever attempted, just as long as I took time off to take her fishing. It includes my father, whose photographic insight made this book possible and who, by example, taught me to carve out my own unique way. And my mother who let me know that this would be no easy task. I thank my sister, who encouraged me to find an avenue to share this precious collection of photographs. I thank my grandfather who taught me courage and contributed his memory of places, people and events in telling the story behind the pictures.

I am grateful to: Phil Stewart, Jo & Tom Swanson, Maria & Charlie Morekis, Marianne & Ward Merrick, Jr., Don Bigot, Jerry Melvin, Claude & Tona Trammell Newland, Joey Reyes, Bill Irland, Mark Shahid, Peggy & Tom Rice, Willie Mae Taylor, Chris Gibson, Dooney Tickner, Barbara & Randy Lykins, Chris Artist, Barbara & Billy Mills, Mark Holderfield, Lili Bass Hill, Christina Tyler, O. T. Melvin, Ernestine Reyes, Julee Dardeau, Captain Jimmy Trammell, Captain Delbert Marler, Danny Cox, Barbara Sullivan, and The Friends of the Destin Library.

In Special Remembrance: Olivia & Arturo Mennillo, Ricky Mennillo, Frank Holderfield, Billy Edgington

Anthony A. Mennillo

HIGHWAY TO HEAVEN

Table of Contents

Chapter One: Arturo 1

Chapter Two: The People 21

Chapter Three: The Fish 31

Chapter Four: The Boats 55

Chapter Five: The Rodeo 89

Chapter Six: The Places 101

Chapter Seven: Famous Visitors 141

Chapter One
Arturo

1

Arturo Mennillo was a professional photographer who lived in the Destin, Ft. Walton area from 1945-1965.

During that period, he recorded the "Emerald Coast" through the eye of his camera.

1925 - 1996

Photography Exhibit

Ft. Walton Beach, 1955

*A*rt, a New York City Lad, was fortunate to be stationed at Eglin A.F.B. where he met and married a very lovely lady from a fishing family. Art was not interested in pursuing the fishing tradition. Instead he followed his life long ambition... Photography.

Arturo captured and preserved the places and people of the Emerald coast area; Beautiful pristine beaches, sport fishing at its finest, founding families throughout their life events, street scenes and celebrity visits - all recorded for history. It is a nostalgic and priceless collection.

A Word From Arturo

Amsterdam, 1976

Saigon, 1966

During the more than twenty years that I operated "ARTURO'S STUDIO", I devoted many hours and much effort to the overall promotion of Ft. Walton Beach and the surrounding area. In the course of these events, I accumulated many negatives concerning the general history of the area and became known as the area's "Official Photographer". In this capacity I had many exclusive photo assignments that resulted in a total negative file of well over 10,000. These negatives represent the only historical record of its kind in existence today.

I left Ft. Walton in April, 1966, as the Official Photographer for the U. S. Embassy in Saigon, assigned to cover the progress of hundreds of military projects. I had intended to complete that first 18 month contract and return to Ft. Walton to reopen "ARTURO'S STUDIO". As things turned out, I had embarked upon a whole new career. It was 10 years later that I finally left Vietnam for assignment in Africa, Iran, Hong Kong, Singapore and a number of locations around the world before finally coming back to the "States"... some twenty years later.

The Family

Tony Learning the Trade

Arturo's son, Tony, borrows his uncle Coby Brunson's hat, rod, and dock to fish in the Rodeo.

Award winning photograph of Arturo's daughter, Carol Ann.

As Tony became older and more skilled, his catch got better, as this fine stringer of chofers will verify, 10/3/52.

Tony was always courteous to the young ladies.

Arturo's youngest son, Ricky, gets dressed up for a date.

Arturo's Artistry

Pristine..... Serene..... Heavenly..... Yesterday

Carol Ann On Dunes

Arturo captures his daughter in a contemplative mood. It is unusual to find a person Arturo's landscape photography. Here he uses Carol Ann to show the scale of the sand dunes for a dramatic effect.

Sunset
"Watch for the green." When far out in the Gulf, on a clear evening, as the sun drops out of sight, a very deep flash of green can be seen.

"Yellow Bluff" Miramar Beach
The only dune within 12 miles of East Pass at Destin with yellow sand. All others are white.

Sunset on Sea Oats

Day's end, in beauty and tranquility...

Sunset On Driftwood

Shadows On Dunes
Hurricane Opal destroyed many beautiful dunes such as these.

Joe's Bayou
Brings back precious memories of the past.

Joe's Bayou "Storm Mooring"
Provides safe anchorage when hurricanes threaten the Pass at Destin.

SEINE NETS

Extinct Species... Netting of this type was the main source of existence for the founding families of Destin, for several generations.

"The purpose for seine reels, as they were called... Our nets were made out of cotton material and with all the fish slime and rubbish that would get in them, we had to dry them daily. Most people have never seen one before." Captain Reddin "Salty" Brunson

Chapter Two

The People 2

Standing left to right: John Cox, J.V. Kirkland, Jake Hogeboom, unknown, unknown, Jimmy Trammell, Gene Marler, unknown, Bruce Marler, unknown, Coleman Kelly, unknown, unknown, Mr. Windes, Cobie Brunson, unknown, unknown **Kneeling:** unknown, Zak Brunson, Bernard Kelly **Sitting:** Tyler Calhoun, unknown, W. L. Marler, Lee Martin, Reddin Brunson, Garfield Taylor

Destin's First Community Center

Jake Hogeboom lent the committee $8,000 to hire Docci Bass to build the first community center, led by Fred Zebre, who was also instrumental in the first Destin library.

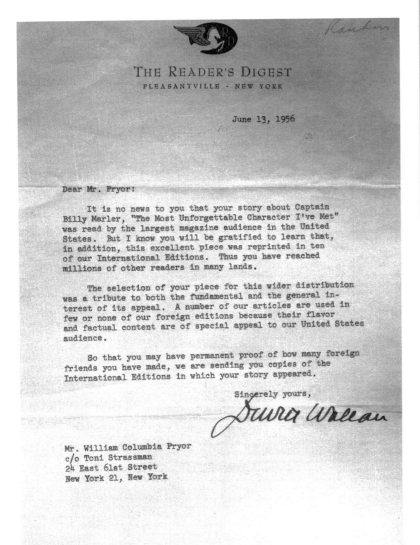

These gentleman did so much for so many. Everyone referred to them as uncle.

Wm. Thomas Marler
"Uncle Billy Marler"

Wm. Columbia Pryor
"Uncle Willy Pryor"

Uncle Billy Marler, established the Post Office, a school, and a church. He began the first Christmas Tree Celebration in 1915 and acted as Santa for the children. He was the "Most Unforgettable Character." He believed that all things were possible if you trusted and believed in God. He also believed that "Fishermen were God's chosen people."

The article "The Most Unforgettable Character I've Met", along with the largest collection of Destin's history, is opened to the public every Wednesday at the Old Post Office Museum. And if you're lucky, Mrs. Willie Mae Taylor will be there to tell stories of the people, industry, and events of Destin's past.

Gran-Ma Destin

A very lovely lady. Grandmother, mother, and great grandmother to many people from the area. She would get up at three o'clock in the morning, cook for the crews and see the hands off to work.

Mattie Kelly

Destin matriarch, Mattie Kelly, took time from her busy schedule, and donned fishing gear to fish in the Destin Fishing Rodeo.

And the Winner is...

Capt. Ben Marler receiving the revolving trophy from Capt. Reddin Brunson. Uncle Willie Marler is looking on.

Elisha Marler, Garfield Taylor, Reddin Brunson, John Cox, and W.L. "Willie" Marler

Paul Roberts

Leonard Hutchinson

*Retired Secret Service.
A man who devoted many hours
to the promotion of the
Destin Rodeo.*

Chapter Three
The Fish 3

Fishing was our Business and our Pleasure!

John FitsHugh, New Orleans on MYSTERY

Otis Elevator Company workers on REVEILLE

Groupers bagged on BARBARA ANN

Ray Deal, Lee Martin and Friends

Ray Deal and Lee Martin, below, displaying a couple of large fish; a copper belly grouper, and a sow snapper.

Captain Dave Marler

Capt. Dave Marler with a couple of happy anglers. The guy at the end must have won the jackpot that day from the smile on his face.

CATCH OF THE DAY

Capt. Chubby Destin of the SHOOTING STAR, with a family showing off their string of fish, 1957.

Kenneth Cary and William Garner displaying a huge grouper.

Stingray

*James Talley,
Charles T. Collier,
C.G. Arnold*

Captain Fred Jones

Weekly Rodeo winner, in the early 50's, Claudine Reed with crewman, Buddy Holley, and Capt. Fred Jones holding fish.

During the late 1960's Fred Jones and Reddin Brunson started the first Cobia Tournament on the Gulf Coast called the Destin Cobia Tournament. It was held out of the East Pass Marina which was built by Capt. Homer Jones and Capt. Reddin Brunson and later owned and operated by Fred Jones.

As legend holds, Capt. Fred Jones caught a 150 lb. cobia using a handline and a butterflied mingo. It was so much fun, a tournament was formed that continues today.

Hobart Reed

Hobart Reed, a great contender, seldom missed a day of fishing during the rodeo.

Captain Bruce Marler

Capt. Bruce Marler and mates, Buddy Brunson and Joel Johnsey, caught the first blue marlin. Legend holds it was caught by Destin's sea buoy.

*Her Majesty
Deep Sea Fishing*

Tennessee group with sailfish on GIBSON GIRL, 10/09/56.

Fishing trip won by the one millionth passenger to board Southern Airways.

Louisiana group on REVEILLE with Capt. Jimmy Trammell, 10/09/56.

Alabama group on MARATHON, 10/09/56.

Howard Marler with happy anglers

Trammell, back right

Debert Marler, far right

Spence Fish House in Niceville

A founding family, the Spences have been in the fishing industry for generations. Tradition continues today with the nationally renown "Mullet Festival" held yearly in Niceville.

Chapter Four

The Boats 4

Boat Building

In the early days, Captains either built or assisted in the building of their vessels. Boats were built at water's edge for ease of launching.

C.C. (Lum) Thompson built many of Destin's fleet fishing boats.

These include: THE CAPT. BERNIE, MARATHON, BARBARA ANN, MISS JULENE REVEILLE, and MYSTERY, just to name a few.

C.C. "Lum" Thompson, boat builder and Capt. Roscoe Mikel, future skipper.

THE FLORIDA GIRL
Capt. Dave Marler was a pioneer in the party boat business. THE FLORIDA GIRL was Capt. Dave's second big party boat.

Uncle John Destin
Master Boat Builder

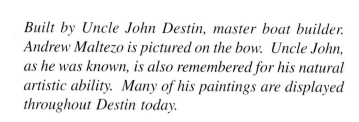

Built by Uncle John Destin, master boat builder. Andrew Maltezo is pictured on the bow. Uncle John, as he was known, is also remembered for his natural artistic ability. Many of his paintings are displayed throughout Destin today.

THE GULF QUEEN

Capt. Buck Destin, owner and operator of Destin Bait Co., would act as a stand-in Captain for the fleet. This was a big help, should an emergency arise, in preventing any fishing group reservations from being cancelled.

THE COURAGEOUS

THE COURAGEOUS, built and operated by Capt. Dave Marler, the first pay faring party boat in Destin.

THE MARATHON

THE MARATHON, built by C.C. (Lum) Thompson, was owned and operated by Capt. Ben Marler. She was later sold to Capt. O.T. Melvin.

GEE EYE

Skippered by several Destin fishermen, the GEE EYE was built by General Sibert as a business venture.

This boat is in Old Pass Lagoon. Notice how high the sand is on Norriego Point.

REVEILLE

REVEILLE was owned and operated by Capt. Jimmie Trammell, one of three surviving skippers from 1950, as of Founder's Day, 1998.

GLORY
Bill (Biscuit) Brown, owner and skipper of the charter boat GLORY.

The Kelly Fleet

Coleman and Mattie Kelly, owners of the Kelly fleet, which included:
MARTHA JEAN, GATEWAY, MISS TEK-NI-COLOR, MISS NEW ORLEANS and others.

BILLY

Barbara June Brunson
Captain Salty's daughter

THE BARBARA ANN

BARBARA ANN was owned and skippered by Capt. Reddin "Salty" Brunson. A living legend, Capt. Salty has devoted a lifetime to the overall promotion of Destin. Respected and loved by many, Capt. Salty, at age 84, was spotted in the spring of 1998 with Capt. Fred Jones, shrimping, crabbing and "jumping" a few tarpon at Indian Pass.

BARBARA ANN of DESTIN, FLA.

"The term, 'Garbo' was derived from the way mates were paid for their services. Passengers would board a boat with a 20 gallon garbage can expecting to fill it with snapper and grouper during the course of the fishing trip. They would pay about $4.00 for a day of fishing. They would then sell the fish and in many instances, make more money than the skipper did for the day's work." Capt. Salty

Family night on the BARBARA ANN, with Capt. Roscoe Mikel at the helm. Capt. Salty's wife, Gladys, brothers, sisters, in-laws and grand-kids all on board. "We would beach the boat. Zak, Coby, and J.D. Brunson would fix the scrunch (crab, shrimp, oysters, scallops, grouper gumbo). My daughter, Jo, and Tom Swanson shucked the oysters. Life was simple B.C." Capt. Salty

The Barbara Ann II
Owned by Captain Reddin Brunson

Sea Queen

Built and Operated by Captain Coby Brunson

THE MISS KATHY

In the late 1960's, Capt. Reddin Brunson and Dr. Joe Wilson added the MISS KATHY to the Destin charter boat fleet. Current rates for a half day were $35.00 and all day, $65.00. The MISS KATHY started charging $65.00 half day and $125.00 full day. That set the pace for more profitable fleet operations.

3rd day, ye 10th of June, 1997

Dear Reddin:

Mate ahoy... This a.m. I'm imbued with memories of Old Destin, at a time when you and I were adolescents roaming the hard white sand beaches of the area, and trusting we'd be lucky enough to evade the dorsal fin of a half buried catfish, which Ed Marler was unfortunate enough to stumble upon, which experience resulted in "laying him up" for several weeks. Such and similar encounters were just one and many travails of our seacoast heritage.

In reality, Destin, representative of the western end of the Choctawhatchee Bay-Gulf Peninsula was a dead end and devoid of the normal pleasure of other settings. With no modernity... accentuated with no amenities such as bridges, roads (streets and highways), electricity, telephone, natural gas, running water, etc. Our options at other engagements were limited: In fact, a way of life had devolved. Nevertheless, modernization of the area would in time emerge with freneticism. But, at the moment in question, progress had been substituted by an unimaginable aura of serenity, tranquility and a natural scenic beauty of "gin" clear Gulf and bay waters, snow white beaches, sea hills and valleys vegetated with a stunted growth of gnarled oak, magnolia, pine, etc. Contrasting with the vegetation, north of the sea hill line, in which latter area plants grew maturely to their prime, in which the boughs of towering pines, were permanently configured to the northwest... so structured due to the almost constant southeast winds. However, climatological vicissitudes meant little, except for the hurricane season when boat owners stood prepared to move their vessels to the safety of Joe's Bayou.

Destin, with its meager population and one "industry"(fishing) offered no opportunity other than joining the fishery: and after a nonproductive season could leave an optimist devastated and ready to pack his sea bags and travel thither in search of "greener pastures." So, in our early years what was one to do except "weather" the consequences, and in our solitude build castles in the air while preparing for the annual spring's "crazy southeasters" and the winter's "blue northers," which only exacerbated an already frustrated insularity. Inclement weather brought fishing to a halt, causing the scanty populace to "hole up" as it were in their "diggings" and indeed it was a welcome sight to sight a schooner dropping anchor in the pass, stimulating some curious Destinites to row out alongside and engage the schooners crew in common banter (fishing). I can visualize the visit... of the "hands" sitting on the cabin trunk, others on the hatch, while savoring the smell of coffee fumes drifting outward through the fo'c'sle's companionway. Or, in the absence of schooner(s) there were the fishermen shanties below the bluffs, on the beach to visit, and listen to the often told peregrinations of Bob Hammock and Bob Shirah as "Knights of the Open Road" (hoboes), as when they rode the "rods" as "rodneys" as the British say, of freight trains from Pensacola to San Diego, where they shipped in a tuna fishing vessel that isolated them at sea on a 45 day trip, and rewarding them with a $400.00 share each. Bob Shirah returned to Destin dressed like a Philadelphia lawyer. If you remember, the period in question was shortly after the bottom fell out of Wall Street (The Big Depression), or about 1930; and Bob's (Shirah) new suit contrasted sharply with the apparel of his contemporaries (shipmates), as the coats and jackets of the latter sported "Liverpool Buttons" (sail twine drawn through both sides of a garment and secured with a slipknot to replace missing buttons).

Bob Hammock was a good shipmate, but a bit "crafty". He was the kind of a guy who had finished the 5th grade and called it his senior year.

To hear Bob (Hammock) discoursing, one would have surmised that he was an associate of the law firm of "Dewie, Mislead'em and How," or a member of the "Utah Jazz". Do you remember when Bob operated the runboat FRISBIE from Destin to Niceville for Claude Meigs? When the FRISBIE was tied-up in Destin, Bob's lighthouse keeped in an old shanty atop the bluff, was once occupied by a Misses Drake... Ed Wells married one of the Drake girls, Alice by name.

Do you remember when Bob Hammock was campaigning for County Commissioner? He wrote his speech and practised delivering it in the bunkhouse. It went thus... "My fellow citizens lend me your ears. I have fought for my country. I have often had no bed but a battlefield, and no canopy but the sky. I have marched over frozen ground till every step has been marked with cunning and deceit. My opponent and present incumbent has been robbing you for the past ten years, now give me a chance... and I promise not to put you to sleep with after dinner speeches... blah, blah, blah and blah." During Bob's campaign he said to my dad, "Odum, have some candy. It's political taffy." My dad responded with, "Why do you call it that?" Bob replied, "Because it has lots of pull."

Take care and remember me to your family... love to all.
Your school and shipmate of yesteryear,

O. T. Melvin

Blessing of The Fleet
May 23, 1958

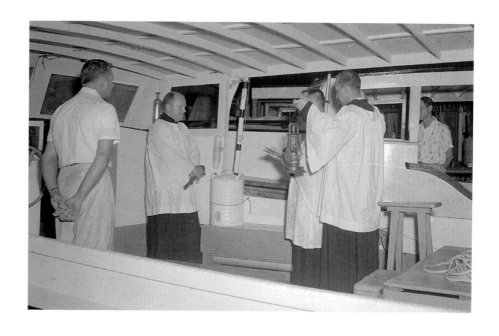

SHOOTING STAR was first build for Capt. Zak Brunson as a commercial fishing boat. She was sold to Capt. Chubby Destin to be included in the charter fleet. The vessel later sold to Capt. David Rojas, who still operates her today as a charter boat.

The Mystery, built by Lum Thompson for Captain Howard Marler
The first full fledge charter boat in Destin, Capt. Marler's legion goes on.

THE DOLPHIN
Owned by Capt. Ed Marler. Originally a commercial fishing vessel, The DOLPHIN was converted to a charter vessel after the success of his brother, Capt. Howard Marler.

THE LITTLE MARTHA
Nobe Tyner from Lauriel Hill, brother-in-law of Congressman Bob Sikes, first came as a pay faring customer. After a few trips, he had Bob Parrish build the LITTLE MARTHA and went into business for himself.

THE GIBSON GIRL

Ronald Gibson, from Cinco Bayou, was a prominent businessman in Ft. Walton. Ronald enjoyed fishing so much, he went into the fishing business and became very successful.

THE SHORTY

Pioneer family and successful businessman, Billy Harbeson, had the SHORTY built by Lum Thompson.

*A tribute To
Captain Johnny O'Neal
aboard the EUREKA*

CAPT. NICK
Owned and operated by Capt. Nick Maltezo, a respected and well liked area captain.

CAPT. BENNIE
Owned by Bernie Henderson.

THE CRISANDY

Day Sailer
Not all boats were fishing vessels. A local group making ready for sail.

The Lost Dutchman

August 1, 1957...
Lost Dutchman was at sea for 54 days, until found by fishing fleet and towed into Destin.

Chapter Five
The Rodeo 5

DESTIN FISHING RODEO

Grand Prize car - October, 1956

Actress, Vivian Leigh promotes the 1955 Rodeo grand prize. She was staying in Destin, while filming the movie, "Threshold of Space," with Guy Madison, John Hodiak, and director, Robert Webb.

Destin Rodeo Committee

W.L. Marler, Reddin Brunson, Cecil Woodward and Charlie Hughes

The Destin Rodeo was first established in 1948 to help lengthen the tourist season, and as a fund raiser for Destin's first Community Center. In 1949, the event lasted the whole month of October with daily and weekly prizes. The grand prize winning catch for the month-long contest was a 52 lb. black grouper. As the event grew in size and popularity, grand prizes ranged from cars to property. Today the Rodeo is host to hundreds of sport vessels and thousands of participants.

***THE FIRST
DESTIN RODEO QUEEN
1952***

*Jean Brunson
Escorted by Larry Hayslip*

Jean Brunson crowns the 1953 Queen, Mary Ann Bush.

DESTIN RODEO QUEEN 1953 Mary Ann Bush

Glenda Harrell, 1955 Rodeo Queen

1956 DESTIN RODEO QUEEN CONTEST

*Tommy Jean Runnels
1956 Rodeo Queen*

Roy Martin

Roy Martin won a building lot on Holiday Isle for this 224 lbs. warsaw grouper. He got down and kissed the ground when presented with the deed on October 9, 1956.

Sgt. Meserbe and Capt. Lawson

Sgt. Meserbe from Eglin A.F.B. and Capt. Lawson won the grand prize with this warsaw grouper in an early 50's Rodeo.

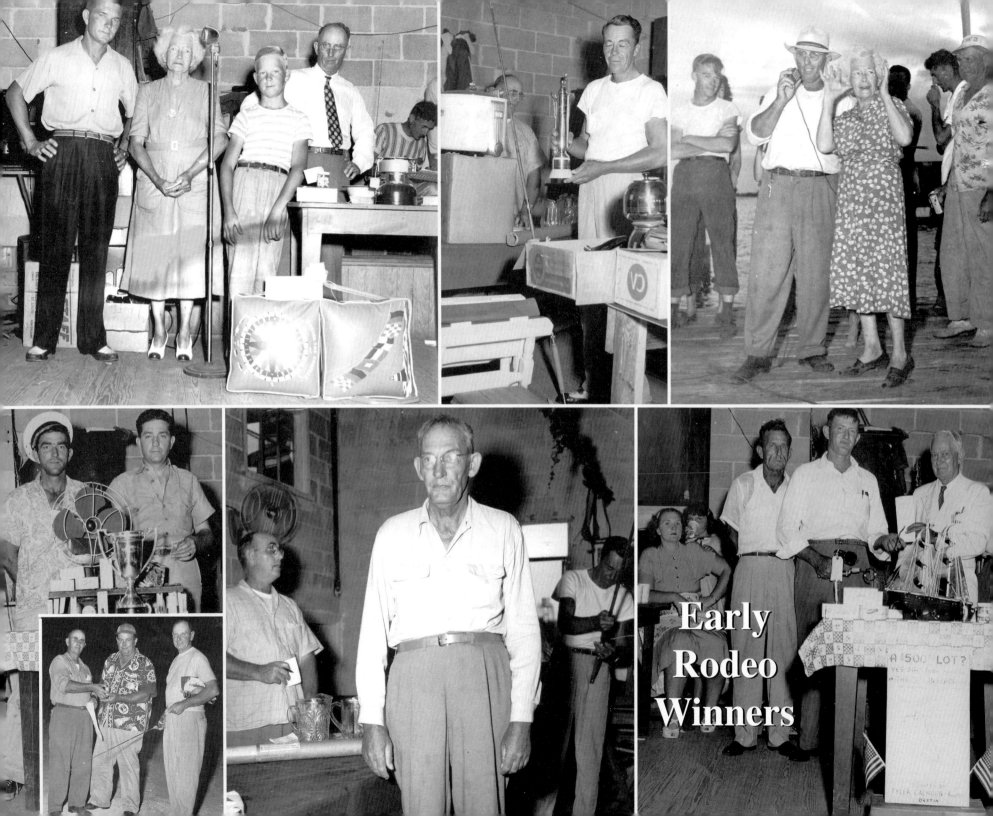

Early Rodeo Winners

Cat-fish

Chapter Six

The Places 6

Today, Destin boasts over 30,000 accommodations.

The Old Destin Bridge

The 65 foot pleasure yacht, (REGINA) sank in this small harbor during the 1936 hurricane. Today, the Destin Coast Guard Station occupies the site where she sank.

The Old Destin Bridge completed in 1934. Notice the wooden pilings.

The Kelly Fleet and Bridge

Arturo spent many hours waiting for the right shot. He referred to this bridge (at right) as "The Highway To Heaven."

"The Patio"

Coleman Kelly's grocery store, hotel, and juke...

The Destin Bridge

The Destin Bridge was the first high-rise bridge in the area. All others were known as draw bridges, with a section either turning or raising for marine traffic.

Destin Harbor (B.C.) in the early 1950's

Destin Harbor in the mid 1950's

An Emerald Coast Deed To Remember
By: James Keir Baughman

Is it mere human vanity, a lofty perception of our importance to the world around us? Or maybe it's just the instinct of self preservation that gives us, for awhile at least, the mute smugness that our own dreams and aims and exploits are somehow momentous, everlasting. It's the slow, steady unfolding of years, the coming and goings of those around us, that unlimbers the knowing, the acceptance that our toils, our moments and thoughts and loves and annoyances will somewhere, sometime slip away, at least from this world we know. Still, there are those who accomplish things so pivotal, so vital, as to be truly unforgettable...or so it seems at the time.

In larger, long settled societies statues of granite or bronze tell their stories for a millennium or two. Here on the Emerald Coast mushrooming, overwhelming growth and the flowing, ever changing flood of new people has buried our short history. Deeds of our early leaders live only in dusty bins of fading records that few ever see or know.

As years have piled up like a stack of old yellowed newspapers, he has become a shining symbol of the loss. When we were so small, so unknown, so insignificant, he built something so big, so visible, so important to our hope of growth and prosperity, his name became a part of it, we thought, for all time. Before the headlines, many of us already knew what he meant to do. Word of mouth has always been a powerful way of linking people and ideas. For months he went door to door, store to store, talking up the impossible, pleading for support and donations, shaping the dream, slowly bequest by bequest, making it our dream.

Lee Martin was one of the two best known saltwater sport fishermen in the area in those years. Not that there weren't a lot of fishermen then. Niceville and Destin were full of them, villages centered around fishing. But commercial fishing was their thing. In Niceville, the boats brought in huge catches from the Gulf of Mexico to be shipped out to fish markets miles

Storm Damage:
April 1, 1957

away. One or two sailing schooners, the old fishing smacks, could still be seen crossing Choctawhatchee Bay in those years, headed through Destin's East Pass to the Gulf. In Destin, commercial angling was for the pleasure of others, hauling vacationers who paid to go deep sea fishing.

The "Newman Brackin Wayside Park" and "Lee Martin Pier" on Okaloosa Island

Lee Martin and Bob McCreary fished because they loved it. With rod and reel, they cast into the surf along the beach, looking for wily, delectable Pompano. Other times they'd be in small boats over grass beds in the bay or bayou fishing for speckled and white trout, redfish and flounder. Bob McCreary's Bay Store, downtown on Main Street, was as well known to the rest of us as our homes. "**HARDWARE & FISHING TACKLE**", the sign out front claimed, but there was far more tackle than hardware. In those easy going years, we wouldn't have been surprised to find a note on the door saying, "**GONE FISHING**". Bob McCreary was hard working, an old Sears & Roebuck manager, but he wasn't above that when the Pompano were hitting. Usually, though he and Lee were out on the beaches when the sun came up, and back again in time for opening. Lee worked for George Alford at Leo's Men's Store, a few doors down Main Street. Fine quality tailored suits and shoes were his specialty. He and his wife lived in a house on Santa Rosa Sound at the west end of town where Main Street's Highway 98 became a highway again.

Early in 1952, radio was a dream, yet just a few months away from Fort Walton, the Playground Area Of Northwest Florida. Crestview had the only station. Television was an unstable flickering, beamed unpredictably from New Orleans without even a hint of local matters. Community tidings were spread by our weekly newspaper, *The Playground News*, one of Florida's finest papers, tempered these 45 years into the powerful *Northwest Florida Daily News* we know today.

Then, it was only the headlines, the news scoop, the reporter's words that brought an idea alive, made it real, important, the harbinger of things to come. *The Playground News* first mentioned it on February 14, 1952. It was Thursday, the day the weekly always came out. A small front page article whispered that Sam Lindsey, president of the Chamber of Commerce had announced the formation of the Fort Walton Pier Association for the purpose of soliciting funds to build a fishing pier reaching out into the Gulf of Mexico. Sam, also a city councilman and later Mayor of Fort Walton Beach, ran an insurance agency. The news report mentioned Lee Martin as the man heading the campaign to raise money and announced that a permit had already been obtained. It said another thing, a thing astonishing to those who did not share those years. The Town of Fort Walton, the reporter wrote, pledged $2,500 toward construction, and agreed to maintain the pier. In fact, the pier was to be built way out on the beach, a mile outside the boundaries of Fort Walton. Fort Waltonites of those early years nurtured the whole area... Shalimar, Cinco Bayou, Mary Esther, Okaloosa Island, Destin...as their own. In fact, it was Fort Walton's Playground Area Chamber of Commerce that worked to build all of the Playground Area.

A week later on Thursday, February 21, 1952, banner headlines blazed across the front page of *The Playground News*, "**WORK STARTS ON $27,000 FISHING PIER.**"

A smaller subhead said, "45 Days Needed To Finish Work; Town To Manage." This time the article named Lee Martin as, "the promoter and fiscal agent for the Fort Walton Pier Association." Theo Staff, head of the Staff's Restaurant family, was named as president. Construction of the city's new $27,000 municipal fishing pier started this week....the reporter wrote, ...at the Newman Brackin Wayside Park, site of the pier. Donations both large and small, *The Playground News* revealed, could be made by contacting Lee Martin at telephone number 2-3611 or Box 57, Fort Walton. The Pier was to be 12' wide, 700' long, with 600' extending out into the Gulf from the water's edge. Keenan Co., engineers for the city of Fort Walton, were in charge of construction.

For the next five weeks, *The Playground News* was silent about the Fort Walton Municipal Pier. Lee Martin, though, stayed very busy making personal visits to area merchants. Shalimar Center, a neighborhood trio of drug/sundry, package liquor, and automatic laundry stores, was owned by my parents E. A. and Iris Baughman. I, the "soda jerk", ran the drug store's lunch counter and soda fountain. Shalimar is two miles from Fort Walton, but Lee Martin came in often on his rounds and my parents donated to the pier fund. He always bought a double dip vanilla ice cream cone. Most men smoked in those years but Lee had a curious habit. He smoked and ate at the same time, exhaling blue-grey cigarette smoke directly onto the ice cream. Nonsmokers would wince to see him do it.

Support grew rapidly. The appeal of Lee Martin's idea was obvious and resounding. Local fishermen and vacationers could fish 600' out in the Gulf waters on the Pier. Surf fishermen could cast out less than 100', wet and often cold, waist deep in rolling waves. "Already, we have classified 16 species of edible fish that are in the waters around the pier," Lee Martin said, "and I believe there are more." The Pier would bring more vacationers to spend money on motels, restaurants, fishing tackle, souvenirs, but *The Playground News* issue of April 17, 1952 brought bad news. "Work has stopped on the Pier," Lee Martin was quoted as saying, "because there is no money to pay the men."

Two weeks later, the issue of May 1, 1952 brought news that was, for awhile at least, a bit better. "Enough money has been raised," Lee Martin

said, "for two more weeks' work." In addition, *The Playground News* reported that the Fort Walton Women's Club had scheduled a "free will offering dance" at the Shalimar Club on Friday night, May 2nd. Donations were for Pier construction. Two things about that event were far from surprising. First, the Fort Walton Women's Club was a powerful voice, a strong social conscience, in the early development of the Playground Area. Second, Roger and Ella Clary, who owned the Shalimar Club, were at the top of the list of early leaders who guided us to where we are today. Their business and social contributions to our area development were, and continue to be, immense. The Shalimar Club, in the tiny village of Shalimar, was one of the most elegant night clubs in the south, with red-coated waiters in formal attire. Andy Griffith, now long-famous as a star of TV and films, appeared there. "What It Was, Was Football," and "Swan Lake" and several other hilarious monologues brought him national fame in the early 1950's. We watched Andy Griffith perform them on the gleaming wood dance floor of the Shalimar Club.

Three more weeks of *Playground News* silence slipped by. Pier construction forged ahead and Lee Martin continued his rounds of fund raising. He'd been joined by his fishing buddy, Knute McCulley, who owned the Pure Oil station three doors down Main Street from Leo's Men Store.

Knute had drifted down from Atlanta. He had fallen in love with the fishing and nature and quiet of Fort Walton, and bought the auto service business. He, too, made calls seeking building funds and his Pure Oil station became a second headquarters for the effort. "A lot of people," Knute recalled recently, "dropped donations off there."

The Playground News issue of May 22, 1952 showed clearly how widespread community support for Lee Martin's idea had become. Mr. and Mrs. H.J. Benkirt of LaRue Frock Shop on Main Street, the reporter wrote, contributed 10% of their last Friday's sales to the Pier construction fund. "The Pier is for all of us." Mrs. Benkirt said, "We hope other merchants will do the same." Lee Martin was quoted, too. "Good progress was made on construction this week," he said, "and the Shalimar Club dance brought us between $200 and $300."

A big two column photo of Lee Martin, Theo Staff, and J.V. Calvin dominated the front page of the June 12, 1952 issue. Calvin was treasurer of the Pier Association. Lee, a slender, rangy man, stood a head taller than the others. The black and white photo doesn't show it, of course, but Lee was always darkly tanned from long hours of fishing in the Northwest Florida sun. His voice was deep-toned, strong. The aura about him was one of self assurance and authority, and his casual dress was often white pants and yachtman's cap. "LEE MARTIN PIER," a headline under the photo proclaimed, Fort Walton Pier Association members, Monday, designated that as the official name for the municipal fishing pier on Santa Rosa Island, *The Playground News* reported. "Mr. Martin has done more than anyone else to promote the pier for the area." Theo Staff was quoted as saying, "The pier is the biggest thing here in several years." The Fort Walton Motor Speedway, the old racetrack for which Racetrack Road is named, scheduled wrestling matches for June 24th with a percentage of the gate going to The Pier fund. And the reporter also noted that the Magnolia Club on main street donated 20% of Tuesday night's proceeds. The Magnolia, located at the corner of Main Street and Perry Avenue where the outlet mall stands today, was the other classy nightclub in the Playground area. "We've already completed 600'," Lee Martin said, "and we're going to add another 150', making it 850' in all. The Pier should be open to the public on July 4th, if weather permits." But on July 10, 1952 *The Playground News* brought bad news again. "$900 more is needed," Lee Martin announced. "The Pier won't open until enough money is donated to back the payroll for two more weeks. Last week," he said, "I had to shell out of my own pocket to finish meeting the payroll, and I don't plan to do it again. A dime, quarter, dollar or five - whatever anyone wants to give will be appreciated." "Presently", *The Playground News* reporter continued, "workman are constructing a 70' "T" at the end of the 710' Pier." It was clear that the extra 150' had been abandoned because of a shortage of money.

"DEDICATION SET FOR MARTIN PIER," blared a two column *Playground News* front page headline, "on Thursday, July 17, 1952."

The following week's issue confirmed it. The "LEE MARTIN PIER" was opened to the public on Friday, July 18, 1952 at 10:00 a.m. The news photo was too big to overlook. It pictured Lee Martin and his wife standing on the long deck, his yachtman's cap set jauntily on his head. He held scissors in his hand, ready to cut the red ribbon that opened the Pier to the public. Mrs. Martin's high heels seemed a bit out of place on the roughness of the boards, but her smile was gracious. Of all the sunrises and sunsets before and after, that day belonged to them. The skirt of her pretty off-the-shoulder sun dress rippled in the sea wind...a lovely breeze, unchanged, these 45 years. She held a bottle of champagne at the ready, determined to smash it over the railing as though launching a 700' ship.

Pastor Johnson Pace of downtown St. Simons-on-the-Sound Church gave an invocation, and Fort Walton Mayor O. M. "Pete" Early made the dedication speech. "It is a real dream come true," Mayor Earley said, "fulfilled by many people. But, it was Lee Martin's hard work that made the dream come true." Theo Staff, president of Fort Walton Pier Association was quoted one final time. "Lee Martin deserves all the credit", he declared. "He got the thing started and pushed it by himself. It is only fitting that it bear his name."

Mrs. Martin, said *The Playground News* reporter, gave the champagne bottle a healthy whack on a corner of the Pier. On the second try the bottle split a concrete block. Then, on the third, the bottle bounced off a post. On the fourth, she grabbed the neck of the bottle tightly and shattered it. "You can see," Lee Martin commented. "This Pier is going to be here a long time."

And so it was. For twenty five or thirty years, more than a quarter of a century, to those of us who knew the truth, it was the "Lee Martin Pier." Hundreds of us, and thousands of visitors, walked its planked deck, delighted in its ocean scent, caught its fish, gripped its rails unsteadily in gusty wind and rain to see the big waves of a coming hurricane. Lee Martin's Pier more than surpassed the dream itself. And then, a decade or so ago, the Pier passed to Okaloosa County Commissioners...in Biblical terms, to those, "who knew him not." Millions were spent on the fancy concrete pier, built anew on the other end of Wayside Park. In their unknowing, in their haste, the commissioners had forgotten all he had achieved...all we had done.

Suddenly, there was a new name, a trendy corporate name...the Okaloosa Island Pier. It is, it seems to this troubadour of our brief history, a bland name, a cold name, a name without flesh and blood, without the toil or hope or worry or doubt that shaped it's sire. It is a name that spews our past out of it's mouth, and violates the tales of what we were, of how we came to be.

There were just 2,388 in Fort Walton in 1950, certainly a few more in 1952, when Lee Martin built our Pier. So many, our elders, have danced their dance upon life's stage and left us to finish our journey alone. There are few, now, to complain. Still when the end is up and the song of the surf rouses the sea air along the beach we might heed their voices if we listen closely. Those of us who shared those years know what we'd hear. "Grant us, at least, our remembrance," they'd murmur. It would be a kind, gentle, unaffected murmur for that's the way most of them were. Our imperious, affluent latter day emigres have inherited magnificence that was not easily earned. In those early years, it was shaped with little money, far more with toil and hope and dreams. Lee Martin's name, today, should stand tall on The Pier. His titan accomplishment was a symbol for all of us, for each and every one of the modest, daily, forgotten labors that shaped our lives together then and built this delightful land we've called the Playground Area, the Miracle Strip, the Emerald Coast.

Lee Martin Pier at Newman Brackin Wayside Park
Santa Rosa Island, Okaloosa County

Grand Opening "Crystal Beach Fishing Pier"
A much needed facility for the area. Built by Bernie Henderson - Managed by Lee Martin.

The Crystal Beach Pier

Lee Martin: First Pompano caught from Crystal Beach Pier.

Built by Bernie Henderson and managed by Lee Martin, who was also the promoter of the Lee Martin Pier. Legend holds that in B.C. (Before Condos) Martin was the best pompano fisherman on the Miracle Strip (now called the "Emerald Coast"). "A lot of folks caught their limits of pompano, cobia, and mackerel while fishing from the Crystal Beach Pier," reminisces Captain Salty.

"Old Marina Point"
When Destin was a small, but proud, commercial fishing village.

Beach Motel Apartments

Shoreline Hotel

*Completed 3/23/57.
The largest luxury hotel of its time in Destin.*

Built and operated By Ernest Shahid.
Ernie entertained dignitaries from around the world.

Grand Opening Gala 4/8/57

Silver Beach Hotel

Silver Beach Hotel, a historical landmark, was built and operated by Mr. Roger Clary and later operated by his son, Michael. It was the first of its kind on the Destin beaches.

"Many people thought Roger was using poor judgement in building a complex such as this on the beach in Destin. It turned out to be very practical and profitable." Salty Brunson

Silver Beach Hotel 1950's, Beach Promotion: Nellie Stallings, Imogene Kelly, Carolyn Vegas, Mildred Stouse.

Mr. Roger Clary
Arturo many times referred to Roger as a man with vision, an entrepreneur supreme, and gentleman who contributed much time, energy, and money to the growth and promotion of the area.

Chamber of Commerce Membership Drive 2/20/57 John Tatum, Roger Clary, Louis Woodham, Nelson Davis.

Mrs. French Brown, Luncheon at Silver Beach Hotel 11/17/50.

Marlborough Cottages
Willie and Sybil Marler managed the fishing rodeo from their office in Marlborough for the first two years.

Florida Girl Motel
Capt. Dave Marler & his wife, Stella, owned and operated the Florida Girl Motel.

Frangista and The Friendship House

The Friendship House is presently known as "Captain Dave's on the Gulf".
In its time, it was the most enjoyable nightspot in the area.

The Spyglass Inn

The Spyglass Inn, located next to Silver Beach Hotel, was one of the nightspots in Destin.

Riviera On The Gulf

"Riviera On The Gulf" known today as Pelican Beach Resort.

Dream's End Motel

The Coastal Grill

A small group of Destin's businessmen, discussing business over coffee, came up with the idea for the first Destin Fishing Rodeo.

Ice House
Two Shaw brothers were owners and operators of Destin's first ice house.

Destin Sea Shells & Novelties

St. Andrews Church, November, 1957

U. S. Post Office

*Jimmy Wise, a mail carrier, built this building and leased a portion of it back to the Postal Department.
Later he became a State Representative.*

Willie & Sybil Marler

Vehicle & gas prices indicate the era.
Willie & Sybil Marler were, also, in the gas business in Destin.

Chapter Seven
Famous Visitors 7

Leonard Hutchinson and Capt. Reddin Brunson shove off.

Governor Collins gets hooked up!

Salty, taking no chances, performs a job usually reserved for a mate.

Capt. Brunson promised and delivered a spectacular catch to the Governor!

The Day the Phrase

"WORLDS LUCKIEST FISHING VILLAGE"

Became Official!

One day, B.C., (Before Condos), October 15, 1956, Arturo got word that Florida's governor, Leroy Collins, would be passing through Destin in route to Pensacola to kick off the Interstate Fair. A governor had never before participated in a Destin Fishing Rodeo. Capt. Salty had a plan. With the help of Rodeo manager, Leonard Hutchinson, he convinced the Governor to take 30 minutes out of his busy schedule to stretch his legs and pose for a few pictures at the Rodeo Docks. Well, Capt. Salty and Capt. Homer Jones readied the first of its kind, newly commissioned trolling vessel, the MISS KATHY, and told Arturo to stand by. The locals were able to maneuver the Governor's entourage to the docks. Legend holds that Capt. Salty conned the governor into taking a ride around the harbor, with a promise of having him back on the docks within 15 minutes. "I broke every rule in the book getting out of the harbor that day," says Capt. Brunson. "Arturo went to work snapping publicity pictures of the governor trolling in the Destin Rodeo. I made one pass around the sea buoy and on the way back in, who would get a strike but Governor Collins, a spectacular twenty nine pound king mackerel, 'Wouldn't happen again in a million years'. Well... When Governor Collins returned to Tallahassee, articles with pictures wowed vacationers from all over the south about the 'WORLD'S LUCKIEST FISHING VILLAGE'.

When questioned, "That's hard to believe, to leave and return to the docks with a mackerel within 15 minutes". The Governor just smiled and said, "Not if you're fishing out of Destin.".... and that made it a little more official...and Destin... well... Destin has never been the same since!

THE Air Force Conducts A Symphony For A 'VIP'..
Photographic TEXT BY ARTURO

The Many Faces Of ARTURO
"The Playground's Hallmark of Superior Photography"

Arturo had many exclusive photography assignments of dignitaries and heads of states from around the world including coverage of four presidents. Of the 50 or so photographs of President Kennedy in the Arturo Collection, only about a dozen have been published and seen by the world. Arturo's Studio plans to publish some of the remaining "Collectors Items" in the near future. Photos - 05/04/62

144

STATE DESK   by Percy Hamilton

Arturo May Better Record When President Tours Eglin

Spectators watching President John F. Kennedy tour Eglin Air-Force Base Friday should not be alarmed if secret service agents collar a small photographer with a large camera.

Their prisoner probably would be Arthur Mennillo of Fort Walton Beach, better known professionally as "Arturo." Arturo, whose audacity is unrelated to his size, may be the only press photographer who has shot two close-up, unposed pictures of a U.S. President.

His startled and slightly amused subject was President Harry S. Truman, when Mr. Truman visited Eglin in 1949. The Pensacola News-Journal published the exclusive pictures. Arturo may try to better his record Friday with President Kennedy. That is where watchful secret service agents guarding the President would get into the picture.

"I've got some plans." Arturo admitted.

A plane load of wire service and national magazine photographers and newsmen landed ahead of Mr. Truman's plane when he arrived at Eglin in 1949.

Realizing he didn't have a chance for an exclusive picture in the crowd of newsmen waiting for the President's plane to taxi in, Arturo crouched on the steps of the dolly which an Air Force crew was rolling out to the plane.

Even to me he has never revealed how he arranged it. I suspect it had something to do with his being a former airman at the base.

Canvas sides of the dolly hid him from the waiting newsmen and secret service agents who parted to let the dolly through.

Arturo gambled on getting the sneak picture as the President came out the plane door. He knew that even with luck he had only seconds before the newsmen and agents below saw him.

He had found out that the president always leaves the vehicles he is riding in first.

This meant aides would not be walking ahead, blocking his view in those precious seconds of shooting pictures from the ramp steps.

As Mr. Truman stepped out of the plane door, he reached for his hat to strike one of his famed "Give 'em Hell, Harry" poses for the photographers.

Arturo fired his camera as the President fumbled with the brim of his hat.

Mr. Truman blinked at the unexpected flashbulb. Glancing around, he spotted Arturo below on the steps.

He appeared momentarily puzzled, then smiled and went into his pose.

The pack of newsmen were not amused and loudly proclaimed it.

Neither were annoyed secret service agents caught off guard. They swarmed Arturo, hauled him off the dolly steps and hurriedly checked his equipment for any possible weapons. They turned him loose, however, after a brief lecture on procedure for shooting pictures of Presidents. Photographers were allowed three shots. All were posed and shot when the agents gave the word.

Arturo got none of the posed pictures. Every time he raised his camera, the irate newsmen clipped him with elbows or jostled him. This left him with a loaded camera when the others were finished.

A wire service photographer's flashbulb failed to fire on the final shot. "Hold it for another one!" He yelled to Mr. Truman. The President already had replaced his hat.

"Please," he chided the presumptuous photographer. That was where Arturo got his second unposed, unguarded picture. And the agents again hustled him to one side for another lecture.

Arturo tried for a third unposed picture while Braden Ball, Pensacola News-Journal publisher, was shaking hands with Mr. Truman. A wary agent grabbed Arturo's arm that time and hauled the camera down.

Arturo didn't get within close camera range of the President the remainder of the afternoon. The agents saw to that!

Emil Holzhauer

Famed International Artist, painting early Destin Harbor.

Arturo was listed in the International Register of Professional Photographers. One day Art got a call from a Swiss art dealer giving him an assignment to locate Holzhauer, take some pictures of current works, and give a general update on the artist, since leaving New York for a small house on Boggy Bayou.

Art completed the assignment and Emil sold a number of paintings. Out of gratitude, Emil offered to paint a portrait of Arturo. Art accepted but had a plan. He hid a 35 mm camera inside the box camera that was to be his prop. The following front page story dated August 1, 1962 from the Bayou Gazette read in bold letters "FAMED ARTIST CAPTURED IN PICTURES" by Jerry Armstrong. Niceville-- During the past few months a most unique story was developed and the culmination is shown below in vivid realism. International famous artist Emil Holzhauer lives in this little city on the edge of a bayou in a rather inconspicuous white house with adjoining studio. It was in this small studio that Holzhauer brought to life a portrait of Arturo Mennillo, Bayou Gazette's photographic director. Holzhauer painted him holding his camera which is probably the best known way hundreds of Okaloosans visualize Arturo, as he is commonly known. What Holzhauer did not know during the many sittings, was that Arturo was shooting the artist in his many moods of creation, as shown below. "I used a 35 mm camera and would wait until Emil had an unusual expression and then I would snap it. Emil was so deep in concentration that he never realized that I was taking pictures of him.

"Emil said he felt some of the pictures were some of the best close-up pictures ever taken of him," Arturo said.

One of the factors which make these five photographs, of the 25 shot by Arturo, so unique is that Holzhauer is so completely engrossed in the world of his painting.

The various moods, expressions and inner feelings of Holzhauer show clearly in the following images.

In the photograph in the lower left, Holzhauer almost appears to be in pain or suffering anguish.

In upper center, he is happy and his work seems to completely satisfy him.

In upper right, very deep concentration is expressed as this was probably a very crucial point of the painting for him. At lower right, the artist seems to be enjoying a private joke as he has somewhat of a smirk on his face.

Another interesting facet is captured in the lower left photograph. A self-portrait of the artist is observing in the background.

"It was one of the most gratifying series of pictures I have ever made," Arturo added.

Captain Eddie Rickenbacher

"Back in the early 50's, there was a group of V.I.P.'s touring the military installations around the country. They happened to be at Eglin A.F.B. A helicopter set down on the parking lot out from my dock. A couple of officers came out and wanted to rent a boat to take these people on a fishing trip. They told me to get some sandwiches, wine and cold drinks and just stand by. They didn't know what time they would get there. When the bus came down the hill around 3 o'clock in the afternoon, there were 16 people aboard. Only 15 decided to go fishing. John D. Rockefellar III, was susceptible to sea sickness and didn't want to get on the boat. Well, we went out and trolled around and caught a few king mackerel and bonitos. The sun was getting low in the west, though the afternoon. People were kidding Capt. Eddie about the seagull story. Everybody has seen the movie, I'm sure. Capt. Eddie said, "Gentleman, it's not a joking matter. But to put your mind at ease, there was a seagull that landed on my head and by the grace of God, I caught it. After you've been on a raft without food as long as I was, anything tastes good." A few minutes later the sun was getting low and Capt. Eddie came up to me and said, "Skipper, let's head in." I headed towards the sea buoy. This drunken skunk came up to me saying, "We're not going in. We're not finished," and grabbed the wheel. Well, I backed away. Capt. Eddie immediately stepped back up and said, "Listen, I told the skipper to go in." This is a quote I'll never forget. Capt. Eddie said, "I've spent the last night at sea I ever expect to, so help me God".
A few years later, the promoter of the rodeo, Leonard Hutchinson, saw this photo and wanted to know were I got it. I told him, "Arturo, my son-in-law at the time, and the boat's name was Barbara Ann. You can see the name on the transom." He took the photo with him. That picture appeared on the front page of the Sunday edition of the <u>New York Times</u> with a story kinda like what I told him. The caption under the picture was what I quoted." **Capt. Salty Brunson**

Movie Stars

Director Robert Webb and party at Shoreline in Destin, Movie "Threshold of Space."
Pictured above: Guy Madison, Vivian Leigh, Robert Webb 09/13/55

Robert Mitchum visited the area in the early 50's to relax and fish out of Destin. Pictured left to right: Red Scourners, Arturo Mennillo, Robert Mitchum, Liza Jackson, and her daughter Liz Jackson McArthney.

Gregory Peck and a lovely lady, Olivia Mennillo, talk movie making at the Shalimar Club. Peck was staying in Destin while doing research on a movie.